Stephen Redmond SJ i                          ... Jesuit Province.
His apostolates have ...included teaching (in both Ireland and
Zambia), writing and composing music. Previous publications
include *So Great a Cloud: A Record of Christian Witness* (Veritas,
2008) and *The Rosary Drama: A Scripture-Based Commentary and
Contemplation* (Veritas, 2011).

# SACRAMENT OF LOVE

## Recalling Text and Verse
## Inspired by the Eucharist

STEPHEN REDMOND SJ

VERITAS

First published 2013 by
Veritas Publications
7–8 Lower Abbey Street
Dublin 1
publications@veritas.ie
www.veritas.ie

ISBN 978 1 84730 514 5

10 9 8 7 6 5 4 3 2 1

A catalogue record for this book is available
from the British Library.

Cover design by Colette Dower, Veritas Publications
Printed in the Republic of Ireland by SPRINT-Print, Dublin

*Veritas books are printed on paper made from the wood pulp of managed
forests. For every tree felled, at least one tree is planted, thereby renewing
natural resources.*

In that this sacrament prefigures our fulfilment in God in heaven, it is called provision for the journey because it supplies the wherewithal to get there. In this respect it is also called Eucharist, that is, beautiful gift, for that is what Christ is.

– Saint Thomas Aquinas

*In grateful tribute to all those who helped me on the way to priesthood and in my life as a priest.*

# CONTENTS

❖ ❖ ❖

# FOREWORD
# 'UNTIL HE COMES'

❖ ❖ ❖

The Christ-Event is from eternity to eternity. Two millennia ago it entered the human story in an utterly unique and defining way: God the Son, the Word, remaining who he was, became one of us and lived visibly and palpably at the crossroads of Asia, Africa and Europe as a Reality 'heard … seen … and touched' (1 Jn 1:1), as a member of a human society and culture, making earth what G. K. Chesterton called 'the visited planet'.

The Visit culminated in three days that Christians accept as absolutely unique in human experience and overwhelmingly important for the human family: the days of the Passion, death and Resurrection of Jesus Christ. The Eucharist came into the world at the beginning of that three-day redemptive and transforming drama.

On an evening of full moon at the spring equinox, Jesus and his disciples gathered in an 'upper room' in Jerusalem. Saint Paul gives us the earliest extant account of what happened: 'The Lord Jesus on the night when he was betrayed took a loaf of bread, and when he had given thanks, he broke it and said, "This is my body that is for you. Do this in remembrance of me." In the same way he took the cup also, after supper, saying, "This cup is the new covenant in my blood. Do this, as often as you drink it, in remembrance of me'" (1 Cor 11:23-25).

The Gift was given. It has continued to be given. There have been so many 'upper rooms': the houses of the first Christians; early sanctuaries; medieval and modern churches; wide open-air spaces like Soldier Field in Chicago and the Phoenix Park in Dublin; the fields of war and the hermitages of peace; the simple structures of pioneer missionaries in the Americas, Asia and Africa; prisons including the dreaded Dachau where Blessed Karl Leisner was secretly ordained and celebrated Mass, and the labour camp at Norilsk in Siberia where Walter Ciszek officiated.

Some mementoes of the Eucharist in time of persecution or stress have come my way: a Mass rock from the Midlands; a chalice the size of an egg cup; a seventeenth-century chalice I often used; vestments from an eighteenth-century 'Mass house'; a tabernacle disguised as a set of dummy books entitled *De Nimia Caritate Dei* (Concerning the Boundless Love of God).

Especially poignant are the 'bare ruined choirs', where the Eucharist once was and no longer is, in Ireland, Britain, North Africa, Turkey and elsewhere. I remember a friend flopping down beside me in a ruined church and saying, 'I like to pray wherever the Mass was said'.

This continuing Gift has been cherished, prayed to, clung to, contemplated, explored, accepted as a supremely important Reality, and made the heart and centre of personal life. It has also, alas, been neglected, misused, ignored, rejected and profaned. It is my hope that this book will convey something of the continuity of this crowning act of providence, something of that witnessing, appreciation and love.

We have God's word through St Paul that the Gift will continue to be given: 'For as often as you eat this bread and drink the cup, you proclaim the Lord's death until he comes' (1 Cor 11:26). Along with St Francis of Assisi we can apply to this sacrament the great promise of the Lord at the end of Matthew's gospel: 'And remember, I am with you always, to the end of the age' (Mt 28:20). Along with him we can celebrate earth as the continually Eucharist-Visited planet.

> Ruins: the grass is high
> here Christ arrived, passed by
> here the Mass was said.
>
> The church across the way
> here Christ comes every day
> here the Mass is said.
>
> Until that secret hour
> when Christ returns in power
> the Mass will still be said.

I pray for all the readers of this book (and for others through them) that the Eucharist may truly be for them the sacrament of Emmanuel, of God with us.

*Stephen Redmond SJ*
*Milltown Park, Ranelagh, Dublin, Ireland*
*Easter Day, 31 March 2013*

# THE EARLY CHURCH

### ICHTHUS AND FRAGMENTS

*Ichthus* is the Greek for 'fish'. Among Christians in the early Church in the shadow of persecution it was a code name for the Lord: *Jesus Christos Theou (H)uios Soter* – Jesus Christ, Son of God, Saviour.

Below is a rendering of part of two early Christian tomb inscriptions, and some early Church 'fragments' combined into a brief Eucharistic creed.

### Ichthus Feast

A feast prepared by faith: a Fish from heaven
caught by a Virgin, to friends given
Saviour's gift: so wholesome, no alloy
Hold, desire, receive in thanks and joy

### Mini-Creed

The Lord who died for us and rose again
is truly here: we praise, give thanks, proclaim
the bread is changed, the cup of life is poured
the Body and Blood received in faith, adored
blessed be God, the Doer of all this
thanks to you, Christ, for pardon, joy and bliss

## MARANATHA

This prayer of Christians in the very early Church, Maranatha, is in Aramaic, the general vernacular of Palestine in the time of Jesus. Its most probable translation is 'Come, Lord', primarily a prayer of longing for the coming of Christ in splendour and power. It was very probably used in the Eucharist which was seen in the early Church as a sacramental anticipation of the Great Return. Saint Paul has it at the end of his first letter to the Christians of Corinth – the letter in which he presents the Eucharist as the continuing proclamation of the One who sacrificially died and would gloriously return: 'As often as you eat this bread and drink the cup, you proclaim the Lord's death until he comes … Our Lord, come!' (11:26, 16:22).

## AMEN

'Amen' is a Hebrew word meaning firm, true, trustworthy, connoting certainty and safety. Said softly, it is like the contented murmur of a child in the parent's arms. It expresses agreement, approval, positive response, a definite Yes. Saint Augustine says: 'To say Amen is to sign your name.'

Saint Paul says of Christ in his second letter to the Christians of Corinth: 'The Son of God, Jesus Christ, whom we proclaimed among you, Silvanus and Timothy and I, was not "Yes and No"; but in him it is always "Yes". For in him every one of God's promises is a "Yes". For this reason it is through him that we say the "Amen", to the glory of God' (1:19-20).

He may be giving us a precious echo of the conclusion of a Eucharistic Prayer in the very early Church.

### Come, our Yes

Maranatha: Come, dear Lord!
and so you did, from Nazareth
to Calvary, to meet your death
to save, atone for sin, forgive
to move our hearts to love and live
You're our Yes, Amen.

Maranatha: Come, dear Lord!
and so you do from day to day
we listen to your word, we pray
and then you come as Saviour-priest
as saving sacrifice and feast
You're our Yes, Amen.

Maranatha: Come, dear Lord!
Jesus, there's another 'Come':
yourself in glory, Risen One
in power and splendour, victory
the Kingdom that will ever be
You're our Yes, Amen.

## SAINT IGNATIUS (D. C. 110)

Antioch, the then splendid capital of Syria, had a Christian community dating back to apostolic times. It was there that believers in the Lord were first called 'Christians'. Its most famous member was Paul. Ignatius was one of its first bishops. Below is an echo from the letters he wrote to various communities on his way to martyrdom in Rome.

### One Eucharist

Every Eucharistic element is 'one':
Eucharist, flesh, blood, altar, bishop, all who come
to share one bread that gives you life forevermore
that saves from death, that brings you safe to heaven's shore
to share the Christ who died for us, the Saviour-Son
raised by the Father, now ensplendoured radiant One

### SAINT JUSTIN (D. C. 165)

This layman, a convert from paganism who died a martyr, exercised an apostolate aimed at educated pagans. A famous *apologia* (explanation) of his is an account of the Mass as celebrated in Rome (substantially identical with our liturgy). This is a poetic paraphrase of his essential teaching in regard to the Eucharist.

> Over the bread and wine he who presides
> gives thanks and then
> the people shout 'Amen, Amen'
> his prayer contains the gospel words that Jesus said:
> 'this is my body' over the bread
> 'this is my blood' over the wine
> 'do this as a making-present of all of me'
>
> And so the food that we receive
> (we who, forgiven, love and believe)
> is the flesh and blood of One both human and divine:
> Jesus' utter reality

### SAINT IRENAEUS (D. C. 200)

Bishop of Lyons, perhaps a martyr. His great work is the *Adversus Haereses* (Against the Gnostics). He presents the Eucharist as sacrifice and sacrament and special pledge of resurrection, linking it with his anti-Gnostic affirmation that material being is a gift of God. This poem is a condensation of the second-century Irenaean vision of a Eucharist related to God-given material nature: interestingly akin to a twentieth-century Teilhardian concept of a Eucharist related to an evolving cosmos.

### Nature and Grace

A sprig of vine yields fruit in course of time
a grain of wheat is multiplied, made bread:
nature and man sharing eternal Good
Passover Supper-room, the bread and wine
Incarnate God: a special word is said
nature obeys: bread, wine to Body, Blood

Nature's still there; we're born, we live, we die
He's there too: the One the Father sent
and keeps on sending, Lover to the core
He ensures that death is not good-bye
in Eucharist He's still our nourishment
to welcome us transformed forevermore

## SAINT EPHREM THE DEACON (C. 306–373)

A teacher of theology in Nisibis (in present-day Iraq) and Edessa (in present-day Turkey). He emphasised the role of the Holy Spirit in the Eucharist. Much of his writing is hymnal, so here is a poetic paraphrase of what he said about the so-great sacrament.

### Spirit and Eucharist

Jesus took into his hands what was only bread and wine
in the Father's and the Spirit's name Jesus made them all divine
he said, 'this is my living body, Spirit-filled, no longer bread'
then the cup of covenant, 'this is my life-blood, for you to shed
do what you have seen me do, do this deed with me in mind
eat my body, drink my blood; covenant that's sealed and signed'

### SAINT CYRIL OF JERUSALEM (D. 386/387)

The Jerusalem baptismal catecheses are a treasure of the early Church. Cyril is generally acknowledged as the author of the Lenten series for catechumens. The haiku below derives from the Easter series for the newly baptised, of which Cyril may have been the original writer and his successor, Bishop John, the editor.

#### 'Bodied' with the Lord

Cana, marriage feast
miracle of Christ a guest
water into wine

Christ our loving priest
gives a gift uniquely blessed
ever more divine

Bread and wine become
through the Spirit heaven's fare
Christ's reality

In this Communion
'bodied' with the Lord we share
Life that is, will be

## SAINT JOHN CHRYSOSTOM (C. 349–407)

'John of the Golden Mouth' (Chrysostomos), patriarch of the imperial capital Constantinople where his uncompromising eloquence made him enemies in high places. His stormy career ended in exile and virtual martyrdom. Known as 'Doctor of the Eucharist', he is much revered in the Orthodox Church.

### Freedom and Love

The Eucharist comes to me: because of this
I am no longer captive, I am free
and so I hope for heaven's promises:
immortal life, angelic company
closeness with the Christ who died
in broken body, crucified
and now a Lover radiant
comes to me in sacrament
O providence! O Love immense!

## SAINT AUGUSTINE (354–430)

Became a Christian after years of philosophical searching and sexual misdoing (perhaps he exaggerates the latter). The most influential Father of the Church in the western Church for centuries – a 'Doctor of Grace'. A voluminous writer, his most famous books are *The City of God* and *The Confessions* – the latter being the most renowned autobiography in Christian history. He presents the Eucharist as the sacrament of unity.

### Sacrament of Unity

The bread becomes his body and the wine becomes his blood
by the word of Him who suffered, died upon the cross-shaped wood

We who desire to live have where to live, by what to live:
his body and blood, the sacrament, the gift He died to give

O sacrament of reverent love! O sign of unity!
O sacrament that makes us one! O bond of charity!

We are the Church, we offer, we are offered, we believe
that through your mercy, Christ our priest, we are what we receive

## SAINT GAUDENTIUS (D. C. 410)

Bishop of Brescia in northern Italy. A renowned preacher and colleague of the great Ambrose of Milan. Here is a paraphrase of part of a homily on the Eucharist.

On the night He was betrayed
a sacrificial Gift is given
He speaks in love, a promise made:
'I'll come to you while still in heaven'

On pilgrim way our nourishment
his Passion's very special grace
helping us go the way He went
until we meet Him face to face

Priests and people: all play their part
a Passion scene is what they see
receiving in hand and mouth and heart
One who redeemed them, set them free

Lord, keep this memory clear and strong
make it our thanksgiving song

### SAINT FULGENTIUS (C. 467–533)

Theologian-bishop of Ruspe in North Africa, much influenced by Augustine. The prayer given here is a paraphrase of part of a treatise.

#### Spirit and Eucharist

Spirit, you filled his Heart with love
so he was sacrificed
now bread and wine await your touch
to change them into Christ

Transform us, Spirit, touch us too
to follow him who died
to learn that all who rise like him
must first be crucified

### SAINT JOHN DAMASCENE (C. 676–749)

Considered the last of the Fathers of the Church and unique in that he lived in a region ruled by Islam and was for some time a state servant of the regime. Like Ephrem, he emphasised the role of the Holy Spirit in the Eucharist, and like him wrote hymns. Below is a hymnal paraphrase of a piece he composed.

> The bread and wine become his Body and Blood,
> how can this wonder be? How is it done?
> The Spirit, Love of Father and the Son,
> the Spirit in whom Love is Personhood,
> this Love inspired the Saviour's sacred word:
> the bread and wine became the Incarnate Lord
>
> The Saviour did not say, 'this bread and wine
> just represent myself as symbol, sign',
> no parable here, not clearly understood,
> he said, 'this is my body, this my blood'
>
> But Eucharist is a true prefiguring,
> in it we share in Christ's divinity,
> we hope for the final gift that he will bring:
> the vision face to face eternally

### *SANCTI, VENITE* (COME, HOLY ONES)

The best-known Eucharistic hymn of the early Irish Church, coming from the Antiphonary of Bangor (now in the Ambrosian Library, Milan) that was compiled in the great monastery on the shore of Belfast Lough at the end of the seventh century.

Come, holy ones, share in the body of Christ
come and receive, drink his redeeming blood
Eucharist-saved, nourished in sacrament
come, let us sing our praise to God

Body and Blood, sacrament setting free
we have been saved, rescued from Satan's pit
given for all, Saviour in sacrifice
he is the priest and he is gift

Come nearer still, pure and with faith in him
let all receive gifts that will save and guard
First and the Last, Alpha and Omega
One who will come, the Judge, the Lord

### *AUDITE, OMNES*

The Antiphonary of Bangor contains a long hymn, *Audite, Omnes* ('Listen, Everyone') in honour of St Patrick. It has been traditionally attributed to Secundinus/Seachnall, bishop and colleague of Patrick, but recently a case has been presented for Colmán Alo, contemporary and friend of Colmcille of Iona. It is a eulogy of Patrick as an evangelist but it touches on baptism ('the bath of salvation') and the Eucharist. Herewith a brief paraphrase that unites the three motifs.

> Like Moses with the manna he imparts the Gospel-word
> richly clad as herald for the marriage of the Lord
> he invites all bath-reborn to be their Lover's guests,
> shares with them the heavenly cup that God in love has
> blessed

# THE MEDIEVAL CHURCH

❖ ❖ ❖

### SAINT FRANCIS OF ASSISI (C. 1181–1226)

By his gospel lifestyle St Francis mirrored Christ to the medieval Church. He still challenges and attracts. His celebration of creation (*Canticle of the Sun*) is the most famous piece of Italian literature next to Dante's *Divina Commedia,* which makes him a saint for environmentalists. He was much drawn to churches as places of the Eucharist. The Testament that he wrote shortly before his death contains a famous Eucharist-Passion prayer and a reference to mystical ('corporal') experience of the Eucharistic Lord. Here is a paraphrase of both.

> That faith in churches you have given me
> moves me to pray in all simplicity:
> 'Lord Jesus Christ, we come beseechingly
> here and in all the churches where you live
> and thank you for that sheer humility
> the Cross whereon you died redemptively
> to save the world, transform us, set us free
> to share your life – what more was there to give?'

A special grace; words cannot cope, they fail:
    a flash of light, a lifting of the veil
    to show what's hidden sacramentally:
    the Body and the Blood – at last I see

## Make a Song. Heavenly Word.
## Holy Banquet. I Adore You

These four pieces are traditionally attributed to St Thomas Aquinas (c. 1225–74) but it is strongly argued that he edited, rather than composed, the Office of the *Solemnity of the Body and Blood of Christ,* which contains the first three pieces listed here (two hymns and an antiphon). 'I Adore You' could be called a love song.

### Make a Song

Make a song to celebrate this Eucharistic mystery
glorious Body, precious blood, the ransom paid to set us
free
Mary's Son, the Lord of nations, Heart of God's own
liturgy
given to us and born for us of Mary ever-virginal
giving us the gospel word to know the Father, hear his call
ending life as priest and gift in one momentous festival

Supper-room and friends together, paschal moon, his final
night
Exodus; the great tradition, legal forms and ancient rite
then he gives himself as food; an act of love, an act of might
Word-Made-Flesh makes bread his flesh: with just a word
the deed is done
then the cup; the wine becomes the precious Blood of
Mary's Son
senses fail and faith alone assures the mind that Christ has
come

Let us therefore venerate this greatest of the sacraments
patterns of the past foretold this crowning act of
providence
let our faith enrich our mind, discover all that's veiled to
sense
To the Father, to the Son incarnate in this mystery
praise and glory, power, thanksgiving, as it was, is now, shall be
to their Love, the Holy Spirit, equal praise eternally. Amen.

### Heavenly Word
You are the heavenly Word with Father endlessly
your life that sets us free comes near its end
you give yourself, dear Lord, as food of ransom paid
while you are being betrayed by a so-called friend

Quickly the deed is done: beneath a twofold sign
both human and divine the living Lord
One of us, Mary's Son, the One the Father sent
companion, nourishment, the price, reward

War with the enemy: come, save, be at our side
dear gift that opens wide the heavenly door
praise to the One, the Three, the Lord who loves to give
who brings us home to live eternally. Amen.

### Holy Banquet

Holy banquet heaven-sent
Christ himself our nourishment
memorial of his passion, of his death on Calvary
Gift to fill the heart with grace
till we see him face to face
promise of eternal life, of future glory

### I Adore You

Deeply I adore you, veiled divinity
underneath the signs I see you are truly here
and to you I surrender, Love so strong, so near
contemplating you, my Lord, leads to ecstasy

Thomas saw your hands and feet; wounds I do not see
Yet like him I call you Lord, call you God, adore
Jesus, let me believe in you ever more and more
Jesus, let me hope in you, love you utterly

Sacrament of Calvary, Lover through and through
sacrament of Easter Day, Gift of living Bread
let me savour your sweetness, purified and fed
giving thanks forevermore, drawing life from you

Now I turn to you in faith: you are veiled from me
hidden Jesus, hear my prayer, give this longed-for grace
bring me out of the shadowlands, let me see your face
in your glory let me find joy eternally. Amen.

### SAINT CATHERINE OF SIENA (D. 1380)

Siena's most famous citizen, mystic, Dominican tertiary, spiritual mother to a religious clientele, adviser to two popes, offering her life for a Church gravely wounded by schism. Doctor of the Church. Below is a paraphrase of some lines of her famous *Dialogue*.

**The Giving God**

I am God provident
I give a sacrament
the Body and Blood of Christ
the God–Man sacrificed
the bread of life, of heaven
my people's nourishment
all this given

The sea is in the fish
the fish is in the sea
so in the Eucharist
I in you, you in Me
the Love that will not cease
the Ocean of peace

### THOMAS À KEMPIS (1380–1471)

Generally accepted as the author of *The Imitation of Christ*, the fourth section of which is devoted to the Eucharist. Here are paraphrases of some lines from that famous book.

**Mass the Gift**
Mass from day to day
Jesus coming, loving, swift
brings this precious Gift

Think of it this way:
Mary's Yes in Nazareth
Calvary: his death

Lord, what can I say?
make of me an offering
thanks, redeeming King

**Banquet**
A perfect host indeed but more than that:
you are the feast itself, our food and drink
the bread and cup of life, the pledge of heaven
the thoughtfulness we simply wonder at
the grace beyond what we can say or think
the love immense, unique, so fully given

## WELCOME, JHESU!

In the medieval Church Holy Communion was very rare among the laity. Gazing on the elevated Host became a substitute for it. Here is a prayer composed in Middle English verse for the practice. (*Schryfte* means absolution. *Howsele* means communion.)

Jhesu, Lord, welcome thou be
in forme of bred I the se
Jhesu! For thy holy name
Schelde me to day fro synne and schame
schyfte and howsele, Lord thou graunte me bo
ere that I schale hennes go
and verre countrycyone of my sinne
that I lord dye there-inne …
but whenne that I schale hennes wende
grawnte me the blysse with-outen ende. Amen.

# THE SIXTEENTH-CENTURY FOUR

❖ ❖ ❖

### SAINT IGNATIUS LOYOLA (1491–1556)

In the early phase of his 'conversion pilgrimage', Iñigo or Ignatius Loyola experienced in 'inward light' the presence of Christ in the Eucharist, an experience akin to that of Francis of Assisi. In Paris, not yet a priest, with companions he pronounced apostolic vows at Mass at the moment of Communion. Later in Rome, by then a priest and with the Society of Jesus officially established, he celebrated Mass, made his formal vows just before Communion, received the vows of his companions and administered the Sacrament to them. The link between Eucharist and vows is surely evident. Sometimes, while saying Mass, Ignatius had a mystical insight into the Blessed Trinity and shed tears of consolation.

> I'm a Basque, once a soldier, a man on the move
> suddenly finding a new kind of love
> Eucharist, Trinity, shafts of new light
> Is all this for peace, for a new kind of fight?

## SAINT THOMAS MORE (1478–1535)

Daily Mass and prayer comprised a regular part of the life of Thomas More. However, it was his custom that before undertaking notably important business he would not only attend Mass but would receive absolution and Holy Communion. Such business had often involved state affairs: supervision of parliament, ambassadorship, chancellorship … He had been a trusted servant of King Henry VIII, whose dismissal of his queen Catherine of Aragon and relationship with Anne Boleyn had distressed him. This, no doubt, had led to his resignation of the chancellorship.

On the morning of 13 April 1534, More attended Mass, received absolution and Holy Communion in Chelsea parish church. He had been summoned to take an oath that day which was against his conscience. An act of parliament had been passed fixing the succession to the throne on the children of Henry and Anne. The act enjoined an oath to maintain that succession. More was willing to accept that succession. However, he knew that the oath was to protect 'the effects and contents' of the act and that the act in its preamble repudiated the authority of the pope in England and Wales. He rejected the oath because the oath rejected the pope without reason. He was imprisoned in the Tower of London. Henry got himself proclaimed Head of the Church in his realm. On perjured evidence More was found guilty of denying the new royal title. He was executed on 6 July 1535.

The Thames was the 'main street' of More's political career. The poem herewith is mostly river-scenic but not its last line: William Roper, his son-in-law, who was with him in the boat going to Lambeth where the oath-taking was in full swing, remembered what More said to him: 'Son Roper, I thank Our Lord the field is won.'

> Sweet Thames, run softly, softly run
> from dawn to noon, to setting sun
> from day to year, from youth to age
> you've been my river, scene and stage
> whereon I've acted out my play
> until this hour, this Lambeth day
> Sweet Thames, run softly, softly run
> praise God with me: the field is won

### BLESSED MARGARET BALL

Margaret Ball, the strong-willed widow of a wealthy business man, ran a household in Dublin which was a centre of Catholic teaching against the efforts of the Tudor administration in Dublin Castle to bring Catholics to heel in accepting Queen Elizabeth's religious supremacy and the tenets of her Church. She instructed her servants in the Catholic faith and sent them out to teach the servants in other houses.

Her house was also a shelter for priests, which meant that at certain times it was a venue for the Eucharist. Her activities led to two imprisonments. She died during the second in the 1580s.

Christchurch and St Patrick's, both quite near
Mass just a memory, so very sad
come to Margaret's house, a priest is here
Mass said quietly and hearts are glad

Dublin Castle kept her in their view
and Margaret kept a watchful eye on them
and God who knew his Margaret through and through
finally said: 'We thank you! Come! Amen!'

### SAINT PASCHAL BAYLON (1540–1592)

Paschal Baylon was the son of sheep-farming peasants in Italy. He became a Franciscan brother and remained a brother though he was offered training for priesthood. He was generally the friary porter and was noted for his love of the poor. The eucharistic Lord filled his life. It is said that one day in 1592, critically ill and unable to attend Mass, he died in adoration, listening to the friary church bell announcing the elevation of the consecrated Host. He is patron saint of Eucharistic Congresses.

A bell that rings
to many at the door
including of course the poor
I'm coming on the run
a bell, just one
calling me, I'm sure
I'm coming, I adore
welcome me, King of kings

# AMERICAN CAMEOS

❖ ❖ ❖

### ANDREW WHITE (1579–1656)

In March 1634, Catholic settlers-to-be seeking the religious
freedom denied them in England, landed on the offshore St
Clement's Island on their way to found the colony of
Maryland. Andrew White of the Society of Jesus, their
'chaplain', described how they celebrated Mass, which 'had
never been done before in this part of the world', on
Annunciation Day and erected 'a great cross hewn out of a tree'
as a 'trophy of Christ the Saviour'. The following haiku is based
on his account.

**First Mass**
First Mass ever here
on the Virgin-Mary's day
freedom coming near

Day of happiness
pilgrim people on their way
echoing her Yes

Cross tree-hewn like His
proclaims Him king in command
Lord who promises

Now we make a start
bless us, bless our Maryland
keep us in your Heart

### SAINT KATERI TEKAKWITHA (D. 1680)

This 'Lily of the Mohawks' lived first in what is now New York State and later in the Great Lakes region. She was intensely devoted to the Eucharist. The poem echoes elements of her culture and background.

#### Lord of the Sun

Lord of the sun and the sky and the fire:
be my one desire
Lord of the earth and the day and the night
be my one delight

Lord of the lakes and the falls and the sea
sing your song to me
Lord of the people I come from: may they
hear you, find your way

Lord of the bread and the wine that you make
into yourself: change me and take
all that I am on to the river
canoeing with you forever

### BLESSED JUNÍPERO SERRA (D. 1784)

Shortly before his death, this great Franciscan apostle of
California finished his final report on the mission of San Carlo
of Monterey. The following poem paraphrases his account of
its beginnings.

Pentecost, seventeen seventy: blessed day
the Spirit is invoked, the Cross is raised
altar and chapel of sorts in Monterey
and Christ in Eucharist is welcomed, praised

An outpost of an empire, royally named
Monterey, the mountain of the king
but now another sovereign is proclaimed
is here in sacramental offering

Some days later, Corpus Christi Mass
a proper chapel now, fit for our Guest
royal procession: King and subjects pass
over ground once heathen, now Christ-blessed

### Saint Théodore Anne-Thérèse Guérin (1798–1856)

Founder of the Sisters of Providence of St Mary-in-the-Woods, Indiana. Pioneer of Catholic education in the then new state. This paraphrasal poem relates to her first visit to the log-cabin chapel of her future mission.

Calvary, Gethsemane and Nazareth:
Trees and timber helped to shape your life and death
and now we find you in a house of wood
in a forest clearing: Body, Soul and Blood
your full reality, all–welcoming
to stay with us, whatever years may bring
thank you, Jesus, Lord of sacraments
Eucharist: crowning act of providence

# THE IRISH HERITAGE

The centuries-old, voice-of-the-people prayers of an Irish-speaking Ireland attest to a vibrant religious culture. They are rich in doctrine, centred on Christ especially in his Passion, attentive to his Mother, mindful of others, intimate and reverent, in touch with nature and integrated into daily life. Here are some of them that are focused on the Eucharist.

Welcome, blessed Sunday, crown of all the seven days,
day of God, of meeting Christ, of thanks and praise

Turn your feet to go to Mass, start to say the blessed word
throw away the chains of sin, look to the Lord

Face that's brighter than the sun, do not keep me on the
rack
Lord, receive my heart and soul, no asking back

I offer my mind with the mind of the Mass
my thoughts, desires and heart
through the prayers of Our Lady this blessing I ask:
a Christian's share and part

A hundred thousand welcomes, blessed Body
the Body that was crucified and slain
welcome, only Son of God, our Saviour
welcome, Lord, again, again, again

I welcome you in love and courtesy
my welcome's like a torrent, full and free
like a father's for his infant in the womb
stay, Lord: in my heart there's always room

A hundred thousand welcomes, dearest Lord
I love you, Mary's Son
make for me a corner in your house
just a little one

Redeeming Father like the ocean sun
forgive us all the sins we've ever done
from heaven, Father, say the healing word
that joyfully we may receive the Lord

I love you now: Lord, stay forevermore
dear heaven on earth, give healing, make me whole
Jesus, my deepest love and faithful friend
protect me now and on that final shore
I say this now lest words should fail my soul
when senses fade and Eucharist will end

We thank you, God of majesty
For giving us, your family
This holy Mass, this legacy
To keep us all sin-free

Two memorials of the penal days that came my way: a chalice
inscribed 'P. Rodachan *me fieri fecit*' ('Fr Rodachan had me
made') and dated, if I remember rightly, 1685; and a Mass rock
at Rahan, Co. Offaly, inscribed 'I M S 1706', and a friend's
memorialist remark.

Sixteen-eighty-five: years swift and few
of royal favour for the likes of you
then Boyne and Limerick, penal night again
did you ever feel the Mass rock rain?
and Fr Rodachan who had you made
who was this man who studied, worked and prayed
to keep the faith alive, who held you up
the symbol of his life, his Jesus-cup?
passed on from hand to hand, from priest to priest
from Mass to Mass, always the Gift, the Feast
from rock to house, from house to church you move
while over you are said the words of love

And now I hold you, say the words, adore
And pray for all who've held you thus before

The yearning of the heart, the thrust of mind
to reach full truth, leave shadowlands behind
the centuries of faith: all that's summed up
in Jesus, Master, Saviour, Word, Host, Cup

*(This poem is dedicated in posthumous tribute to
Séamus Dunican, parish priest of Rahan)*

**Bodenstown, Co. Kildare**
Dated medievally
once Knights Templar property
now a ruin, graves around
at times a place alive with sound
of speeches full of history
of Ireland fighting to be free

We stood in ruined Bodenstown
Eamon Byrne, my friend, knelt down
(in politics not interested)
'I like to pray where Mass was said'

*(Dedicated to the memory of Eamon Byrne)*

# THE NINETEENTH CENTURY

### THE EUCHARIST DOWN UNDER

Many Irish who were convicted of involvement in the 1798 rising were sent to Australia where the British were developing a colony. Three of the convicts were priests, one of them James Dixon. He was given a conditional release so that he could minister to Catholics. He said his first 'regulated' Mass in Sydney on 15 May 1803. This poem envisages him at prayer.

Lord, to-morrow I begin
I'll have a chalice made of tin
work of a convict: all for free
bless him for his piety
I'll have vestments that are made
out of curtains old and frayed

Who'll be there? Well, Catholics
mostly those whose politics
brought them here across the sea
guests of Georgian majesty
and of course there'll be police
custodians of British peace

the rule-book says it's up to me
to maintain propriety

Who'll be there? Well, You will, Lord
when the consecrating word
is said by me, James Dixon, priest
you'll be sacrifice and feast
all of us welcomed, cherished, free
guests of Another Majesty

So to-morrow I'll begin
Lord, come in, come in, come in

### BLESSED JOHN HENRY NEWMAN (1801–90)

A leading member of the Oxford Movement, which advocated a Catholic interpretation of Anglican doctrine. He became a Catholic and subsequently an Oratorian and cardinal. His emphasis on the role of the laity in the Church foreshadowed the Second Vatican Council. He was rector in the 1850s of the Catholic University in Dublin, as well as being a voluminous writer. The first poem is based on a passage from his novel *Loss and Gain*. He was noted for saying Mass raptly and rapidly. The second poem is a paraphrase of a prayer of his.

#### Swift Lord

In the Mass the Lord is present: angels bow
in the Mass He's present in the here and now
instruments of sacrifice: they are the Lord's
bread and wine receive his very simple words
they swiftly go and so it was in Galilee
with Jesus swiftly passing, saying 'come to me'
He swiftly goes and swiftly visits day by day
we too make haste and bow our heads, adore, obey

#### Self-offering

Lord, you're offered in the Mass engracing all our days
you're the one who intercedes, a priest forever living
in turn I offer you myself in thanks, in utter giving
you bought me by your dying
let me complete the buying
by act and deed, so that I'll live in you in strength and
praise

## THE ARK OF KILBAHA

This was 'something like a sentry-box' on a shoreline in southwest Co. Clare in which the local parish priest Michael Meehan (d. 1878) said Mass for a congregation exposed to all weathers. He had been repeatedly refused a site for a church by the hard-nosed estate manager of a hands-off absentee landlord. This memorial of faith is in Moneen Church.

> The land is ruled by bigotry
> and so beside Kilbaha quay
> it stands in faith, hope, charity
> to house the Lord of land and sea

## HOUSE MASS

Aloysius O'Kelly painted his remarkable *Mass in a Connemara Cabin* in 1883. It conveys an ambience both religious and social. Below is a description and reflection.

A dresser, delph, a basin and a butter-churn
a lamp, thatched ceiling, picture of the Sacred Heart
a kitchen where you'd eat and chat and dance and sing
but nothing of that now: a table draped with art
missal, a gilded chalice shines, two candles burn
the priest so young (his coat and top-hat on a chair)
has celebrated holy Mass and turns to bless
the Connemara folk who've shared his Offering
already placed by him in Christ's own priestly prayer
all eighteen on their knees but what is in their mind?
deep-down faith of course and hope of happiness
that God will surely give but there are fears to face
eviction, famine, exile, flight across the sea
I seem to hear a sacred Voice: 'they're good and kind
I take to them, I'll give them lots of love and grace
they're like the folk I knew and loved in Galilee'

### SAINT THÉRÈSE OF LISIEUX (1873–97)

Through the publication of her *Little Way* writings, this hidden Carmelite became immensely popular and influential in the Church. Doctor of the Church and patron saint of Catholic missionary apostolate. The following is a paraphrase of a poem of hers in which she delights in being sacristan.

Let me be the key that opens wide your door
let me be the light announcing you are here
let me be the flame, a message from your Heart
a text of love, a signal strong and clear

Make me altar-stone and make me altar-cloth
(Mother in a cave, a Baby rocked to rest)
let me shine in gold, a monstrance, paten, cup
and there you'd be my loving Lord and Guest

Blessed chosen wheat that grew in God's own fields
blessed chosen grapes matured by God's own sun
now they're bread and wine awaiting words of love
transform me, Lord, with them and make us one

# THE TWENTIETH CENTURY

### BLESSED CHARLES DE FOUCAULD (1858–1916)

The wayward French officer who became a Eucharist-centred hermit in the Sahara desert. He hoped by prayer and charity to attract Muslims to the Christian gospel. Their religious example had helped him in his own conversion. He died (it is claimed, accidentally) by gun-shot when bandits raided his hermitage. Here is a paraphrase of a prayer of his.

#### Desert Lord

Jesus, you are here, my Lord, my All
as fully as you were in Galilee
in the holy house, with friends in Bethany
with men who left their nets, obeyed your call
you are here in Eucharist with me

In you, through you, for you, desert Lord
give all of us the living Bread that's you
nourishing, transforming through and through
across the world may It be loved, adored
with Heart consoled, making our hearts all new

### WILLIE DOYLE (1873–1917)

This Irish Jesuit, already leading a life of great penance, ardent zeal and continual prayer, became a legend of courage and devotion as a chaplain in the First World War. The following is a paraphrase of part of a letter of his.

#### Mass with the Dead

Not far away the battle-din
tiny altar: biscuit tin
congregation all around
quiet, silent, not a sound
as if they were intent to hear
the words of Eucharist loud and clear

They all are dead: both foe and friend
man-made enmity at an end
some foul, corrupt; others seem
to be asleep, perhaps in dream

I lift the Host, I welcome Christ
they've too been offered, sacrificed
for what? for what? I look about
for what? for what? I want to shout
when will this war, this folly cease?
I pray to Jesus: give them peace

I give the blessing: Eucharist ends
one last look: good-bye, my friends
please God, we'll meet in heaven again
Amen, amen, amen, amen

### SAINT EDITH TERESA STEIN (1891–1942)

The German Jewish intellectual who became a Catholic and a Carmelite. She was a victim of the horrific Nazi 'Final Solution' in Auschwitz in August 1942. Below is an adaptation of part of her 'The Prayer of the Church' and a paraphrase of a prayer of hers.

### New Passover

Passover bread and wine transformed by Christ
into himself as nourishment
into himself as sacrificed
the Church begins new life, new covenant

### Dawn Passover

A little bread, a little wine
beneath this new Passover sign
your Body, Blood and Soul unite with mine
you feed me every day at dawn
you swiftly come, you're swiftly gone
the seed you sow in love remains, lives on
to change this dust-thing through and through
to make it more and more like you
preparing it for glory, ever new

### VENERABLE EDEL QUINN (1907–44)

A young woman of frail health, personal charm and heroic commitment who was a Legion of Mary envoy in Mauritius and mainland Africa from 1936 to 1944. The following prayer is an adaptation of some personal notes.

### Adore with Jesus

Jesus, let me be more and more in your company
as you adore your Father in this Sacrament you bring
unite with me in Eucharist in thanks for everything
Mother Mary, full of grace, pray and adore for me

### PIERRE TEILHARD DE CHARDIN (1881–1955)

This Jesuit palaeontologist combined his faith in the Eucharist with a belief that the universe was evolving towards what he called 'Omega Point'. He saw the eucharistic Lord as the 'diviniser' of this process and every consecration in the Mass as an event directed towards consecration of the cosmos. Below is a paraphrase of a sixteenth-century prayer that he associated with his celebration of Mass, and a prayer paraphrase of his thoughts.

#### The Enclosing Heart

Lord, enclose me in your Heart deep-down,
through and through
keep me there, transform my being, set my heart on fire
lift me into all you are, all that you desire
Jesus, let me lose myself, let me live in you

#### The Cosmic Christ

Lord, I come to consecrate the bread
I think of what Augustine said:
'God did not create and go away'
you are a Presence come to stay
from Mass to Mass embracing, radiant
world-consecrating sacrament
God-one-of-us, received and sacrificed
risen, transfigured, cosmic Christ

Thanks for your call to play a special part
in all of this, to share your Heart

### THOMAS MERTON (1915–68)

Having converted to Catholicism, Merton became a Cistercian at the Abbey of Our Lady of Gethsemani in Kentucky. Combining monastic life with social awareness and a notable literary output, he was probably the best-known Catholic monk of his time. Here is a haiku adaptation of part of his *The Living Bread*.

**The Living Bread**

Thank you for this Bread
continuing love-story
life, death, Easter Day

Hearing what you said:
'come, blessed, into glory
I'm the light, the way'

God and Mary's Son
coming for me, for others
change us through and through

Bind us into one:
family, sisters, brothers
all alive in you

## SIR ALEC GUINNESS (1914–2000)

This brilliant stage and movie star became a Catholic in 1956. 'Like countless converts before and after me, I felt that I had come home and known the place for the first time.' Here are verse accounts of two experiences of his that are related to the Eucharist and described in his autobiography *Blessings in Disguise*.

### Dawn Eucharist

The rising sun: a glory red and white
the open door: the church is filled with light
the tinkling bells, the monks, the whispered word
sheer adoration: eucharistic Lord
I sensed God's presence: powerful, radiant
in church, in world, in prayer, in sacrament

### Kingsway Run

Crowded Kingsway: sudden surge
more than just a passing whim
a deep ecstatic joyful urge
to visit Him

I ran, and maybe someone said:
'there's a lover running late
with only one thing in his head –
to keep a date'

How right he'd be: a brilliant guess
church of Cecilia, Anselm
there in utter blessedness
lost in Him

I like to think that on that day
the street outside was my King's Way

### John Cardinal O'Connor (1920–2000)

From Advent 1993 to Advent 1994, the Cardinal Archbishop of New York gave a series of sermons or meditations on the Catechism of the Catholic Church. On Easter Sunday his theme was the Eucharist. What follows is a paraphrase of some of his thoughts.

#### Continuum of Love

Thank you, Lord, that you have made me special
that we can meet in breaking of the bread
thanks for the grace to offer and receive you
the Christ who died, now risen from the dead

Every Mass is Calvary made present
where it's said another Supper-room
every Mass a sacramental Easter
Christ all the time: Presence, Delight, Perfume

Christ all the time: Emmanuel, God with us
always present, always on the move
thanks for this pledge of joy beyond all telling
thanks for yourself: continuum of love

# THEOLOGIANS, COUNCILS, POPES

### HUGH OF SAINT VICTOR (D. 1141)

Named from the Augustinian priory in Paris where he taught and was known as 'the second Augustine'. He is an intellectual bridge figure between the great Bishop of Hippo Regius and St Thomas Aquinas. Here is an excerpt from his *Sacraments of the Christian Faith*.

Through the sanctifying words the true substance of bread and wine is changed into the true body and blood of Christ. Substance is changed into substance: all that remains is the appearance of bread and wine ... The sacrament of the body and blood of Christ ... is completely unique because from it comes all sanctification. For this sacrificial gift offered once for the salvation of the world empowered all preceding and consequent sacraments: from it they were to sanctify all who were to be set free.

### SAINT ALBERT THE GREAT (D. 1280)

This Dominican teacher of philosophy, theology and natural science was a 'star' of medieval scholarship. He is the patron saint of scientists. His *Mystery of the Mass* has been called 'the most beautiful [book] ever written' on the subject. Here is a paraphrase of part of its prologue.

### Divine Good

Good that's from God, the gift of the Lord
invited, awaited, illumined by word
in sacrament present and offered and given
grace in abundance, a foretaste of heaven
cascade of goodness poured out in the Mass
alleluia, hosanna, gratias, gratias!

## SAINT THOMAS AQUINAS (C. 1225–74)

This glory of the Dominicans and a 'great' in the history of philosophy and theology had immense influence on the Council of Trent in its teaching on the Eucharist. More recent teaching bears his imprint. Here is the text from the third part of his *Summa Theologica*.

In that it is a memorial of the Lord's Passion which was a true sacrifice, this sacrament is called a sacrifice. As a sign of Church unity it is called a communion: it unites us with Christ, we share in his humanity and divinity, we are united to one another. In that this sacrament prefigures our fulfilment in God in heaven, it is called provision for the journey because it supplies the wherewithal to get there. In this respect it is also called Eucharist, that is, beautiful gift, for that is what Christ is.

The presence of the true body and blood of Christ in this sacrament cannot be discovered by sense or intellect but only by faith which is based on authority … This presence is in keeping with the perfection of the New Law. The sacrifices of the Old Law contained the true sacrifice of Christ's Passion only figuratively. The sacrifice of the New Law needed to have something more: it should contain not only in sign and figure but in very truth the Christ who suffered. And so the sacrament which really contains Christ perfects all the other sacraments in which the power of Christ is shared.

This sacrament is in harmony with the love of Christ, whereby for our salvation he took to himself a true body of our nature. Friends love to be together, so he promises his bodily presence to us … On our pilgrimage he does not deprive us of his bodily presence but joins himself to us in this sacrament through the reality of his body and blood. And so this sacrament, because of such a close union of Christ with us, is a sign of supreme love and an uplifting of our hope.

The conversion or change (of the substance of bread and wine into the substance of the body and blood of Christ) is not like natural change but is entirely supernatural, brought about only by divine power … God is infinite act … And so God's action extends to the entire nature of being.

God is able not only to bring about formal change (that is, the succession of different forms in the same subject) but also the change of the whole being – that is, the change of the whole substance of one thing into the whole substance of another, and this is done by divine power in this sacrament.

## THE COUNCIL OF TRENT
### (1545–47. 1547–48. 1551–52. 1562–63)

This Council restated and clarified Catholic doctrine in response to the emerging Protestant challenges and initiated some much-needed reforms in the Church. It addressed the subject of the Eucharist in three of its four sessions. Below is the Council text (slightly condensed).

Our Saviour instituted this sacrament when he was about to leave this world and go to the Father. In it he poured out the treasures of his love for us. He commanded that in receiving it we celebrate a memorial of himself and proclaim his death until he comes in judgment.

He was to offer himself to the Father on the altar of the cross in death for our redemption. But his priesthood was not to end by death so at the Last Supper he left his Church a visible sacrifice (such as human nature demands). By that sacrifice the sacrifice of the cross was to be re-presented and memorialised to the end of the world and its power brought to bear on the forgiving of our sins.

Under the appearance of bread and wine he offered his body and blood to the Father and gave his body and blood to his apostles. By the words 'do this in remembrance of me', he ordained them priests and commanded them and their successors in the priesthood to make the same offering.

The faith has always been in the Church of God: that immediately after the consecration the true body of our Lord and his true blood exist under the appearance of bread and wine along with his soul and divinity. By the consecration occurs a conversion of substance of bread into the substance of his body and of the substance of wine into the substance of his blood. After the consecration of the bread and wine our Lord Jesus Christ, true God and truly one of us, is truly, really and substantially contained under the appearance of these natural things.

In the sacrifice that occurs in the Mass the Christ who offered himself with the shedding of his blood on the cross offers himself in sacrifice without the shedding of his blood. There is one and the same victim, now offering through priestly ministry, who then offered himself on the cross. The only difference is the mode of offering.

Christ wanted this sacrament to be our spiritual nourishment and the remedy to heal us of our daily faults and preserve us from mortal sins. He also wanted it to be the promise of our future glory and the symbol of that one body of which he is the head and wanted us, as members of that body, to be very closely united in faith, hope and love.

The Council urges all Christians to believe in and venerate the Eucharist – to have that faith and devotion and spirit of worship with which they can frequently receive the Bread as their spiritual life and health – as their strength in their pilgrimage, whereby they can reach their heavenly homeland to experience the same Bread completely revealed which they now experience sacredly veiled.

## THE SECOND VATICAN COUNCIL (1962–65)

The main objectives of this Council, convoked by Blessed Pope John XXIII, were to present the Catholic faith in contemporary terms in a way that would help the faith life of Catholics and the outreach of the Church and to advance the cause of Christian unity. The Council emphasised the Eucharist as the dynamic heart of the Church, with a special highlighting of the vocation and priesthood of the laity and their role in this sacrament of sacraments. Here is a summary of its teaching.

> In regard to the Eucharist, the Council restated the traditional teaching on the essentials: Christ present, Christ sacrificing and sacrificed, Christ nourishing. The other sacraments cohere with and converge on the Eucharist (an echo of St Thomas Aquinas and Hugh of St Victor). This sacrament contains all the good of the Church: Christ himself (an echo of St Albert) and in it the covenant between God and humanity is renewed.
>
> By baptism the laity share in the priesthood of Christ. This is a true priesthood, though essentially different from the priesthood conferred in Holy Orders. The Eucharist is a very special source of grace and holiness and praising of God, of that love which is the heart of the lay apostolate. It is the beginning and fulfilment of all evangelisation. It is appropriate that the laity should unite all that they do and endure 'in the Spirit' with their offering of Christ in the Eucharist. By their Christian commitment in so many places and environments they consecrate the world to God.
>
> The Council says in effect that the baptised laity are called to be important partakers in the renewal of the covenant between God and humanity, in the Mass on the altar of the world.

## SAINT LEO THE GREAT (POPE 440–61)

Pope at the time of the demise of the Roman empire in western Europe. Renowned for his Christ-focused sermons and for his decisive defence of the integral humanity of the Lord in his *Tome of Leo*, in which he affirmed two natures, divine and human, united with and distinct from each other, in one divine Person. The Council of Chalcedon (451) acclaimed the Tome ('Peter has spoken through Leo') and issued a definitive declaration that was in keeping with it. He was very much a pope of the Incarnation.

> The Lord said, 'unless you eat the flesh of the Son of man and drink his blood, you have no life in you'. So you should communicate at the sacred table without any doubt whatsoever concerning the truth of the body and blood of Christ … Sharing in the body and blood of Christ does nothing else than this: that we are changed into what we receive and that in everything we manifest him in whom and with whom we have died and been buried and raised.

## SAINT GREGORY (POPE 590–604)

He was pope at a time when various jurisdictions had replaced the Roman empire in many tracts of Europe and much of the continent was 'mission territory'. His most famous missionary thrust was to Saxon England. This 'servant of the servants of God', as he liked to call himself, was a shaper of the Roman liturgy and a prolific writer with interests ranging from doctrine to administration of papal estates.

This sacrificial gift ... renews in a sacred rite the death of the Only-Begotten. Risen from the dead, he no longer dies and death has no more power over him (Rm 6:9). Nevertheless, living immortally and incorruptibly, he immolates himself again for us in this rite of sacred oblation. There his body is received, his flesh is shared, his blood is poured, no longer into the hands of unbelievers but into the mouths of those who do believe. And so let us consider what kind of sacrifice this is for us, which to release us from sin always portrays the passion of the Only-Begotten.

## Saint Pius X (Pope 1903–14)

He issued an important decree regarding the reception of the Eucharist. Its background was theological debate concerning a disposition required for frequent and daily Communion with some moralists taking a very strict stance. The decree forbade any such future debate. In a later decree, Pius authorised Communion for young children who could distinguish between the Eucharistic species and ordinary bread.

Frequent and daily Communion is to be accessible to all the faithful of Christ of whatever class or circumstances, so that no one who approaches the holy table in the state of grace and with a right and religious attitude can be prevented from so doing.

A right attitude means this: that the person approaching the holy table should not do so for the sake of (mere) use or out of vanity or for human reasons but should wish to do what pleases God, to be united more closely in love with God and to avail of that divine medicine for his/her weaknesses and defects.

It is very desirable that those availing of frequent and daily communion should be free from at least fully deliberate venial sins and disposition towards them. Nevertheless, it suffices that they be free from mortal sins and have the resolve of never sinning in future … Care is to be taken that there is a diligent preparation for Holy Communion and suitable thanksgiving afterwards.

## BLESSED JOHN PAUL II (POPE 1978–2005)

Karol Wojtyla of Poland was the first non-Italian pope since the sixteenth century. He was also the most travelled and publicised pope in history, becoming a dynamic world figure. He played a major role in the collapse of the Soviet communist empire and was a tireless apostle of Christian humanism, proclaiming the God-given dignity and worth of every human individual from conception to death and beyond. He called himself 'a witness to hope'. His last encyclical, *Ecclesia de Eucharistica*, was on the Eucharist. The following are highlights from that encyclical, along with an excerpt from an apostolic letter.

At every celebration of the Eucharist we are spiritually brought back to the paschal Three Days: to events of the evening of Holy Thursday, to the Last Supper and to what followed it … In this gift of the Eucharist Jesus Christ entrusted to his Church the perennial making present of this paschal mystery. With this he brought about a mysterious 'oneness in time' between that Three Days and the passage of the centuries. The thought of this leads us to profound amazement and gratitude … This amazement should always fill the Church assembled for the celebration of the Eucharist … I would like to rekindle this Eucharistic amazement.

The Eucharist is a true banquet in which Christ offers himself as our nourishment … The 'banquet' always remains a sacrificial banquet marked by the blood shed on Golgotha … [At the Last Supper] Jesus made sacramentally present his sacrifice which would soon be offered on the cross for the salvation of all … [The Eucharist also] makes present the mystery of the resurrection which crowned his sacrifice. It is as the living and risen one that Christ can become in the Eucharist the 'bread of life' and the pledge of our bodily resurrection at the end of the world.

Christ walks beside us as our food and strength for the journey and enables us to become, for everyone, witnesses to hope … making his presence in nourishment and sacrifice the promise of a humanity renewed by his love … The Eucharist is always in some way celebrated on the altar of the world. It unites Heaven and Earth. It embraces and permeates all creation.

Mary is a 'woman of the Eucharist' in her whole life … The Eucharist, like Mary's Canticle, is first and foremost praise and thanksgiving … The Magnificat expresses Mary's spirituality … The Eucharist has been given to us so that our life, like Mary's, may become a Magnificat.

## Apostolic Letter

The Church and the world have a great need for Eucharistic worship. Jesus awaits us in this sacrament of love. Let us not refuse the time to go and meet him in adoration, in contemplation full of faith, and open to make amends for serious offences and crimes of the world. Let our adoration never cease.

Night of Pasch and day of death and Easter dawn
present still in Eucharist-reality
Christ who suffered, Christ now risen, radiant
the world his altar, world-embracing sacrament
Emmanuel, God with us, as we journey on
towards the joy, the vision that will ever be

## BENEDICT XVI (POPE 2005–2013)

Pope John Paul II died halfway through the Year of the Eucharist he had proclaimed. He was succeeded by Joseph Ratzinger, distinguished theologian, Prefect of the Congregation for the Doctrine of the Faith, former Archbishop of Munich. Here are excerpts from his first encyclical, *Deus Caritas Est*.

By contemplating the pierced side of Christ, we can understand the starting point of this encyclical letter, 'God is Love'. It is there that the truth can be contemplated. It is from there that our definition of love must begin. In this contemplation the Christian discovers the path along which his/her life and love must move.

Jesus gave this act of oblation [on the Cross] an enduring presence through his institution of the Eucharist at the Last Supper … The Eucharist draws us into Jesus' act of self-oblation. More than just statically receiving the incarnate Word, we enter into the very dynamic of his self-giving. The imagery of marriage between God and Israel is now realised in a way previously inconceivable: it had meant standing in God's presence, but now it becomes union with God through sharing in Jesus' self-gift, sharing in his body and blood …

Union with Christ is also union with all those to whom he gives himself. I cannot possess Christ just for myself; I can belong to him only in union with all those who have become, or who will become, his own … Here the usual contraposition between worship and ethics simply falls apart. 'Worship' itself, Eucharistic communion, includes the reality both of being loved and of loving others in turn. A Eucharist which does not pass over into the concrete practice of love is intrinsically fragmented. The Lord encounters us ever anew, in the men and women who reflect his presence, in his word, in the sacraments and especially in the Eucharist.

Eucharist-Lord, I've always known
that you create a bond with me
thanks for that but let me see
that you are bonding me and others
so that we are sisters, brothers
and love may have its rightful place
that we may see in every face
Eucharist-Lord, your very own.

# AUTHOR'S MEMORIES

### Dublin
### (International Eucharistic Congress, 1932)
I was with my father there that lovely summer day
Fifteen Acres, Phoenix Park, a million people pray
colonnade and sanctuary, white against the green
an aeroplane roars overhead, intruding on the scene
Pope Pius speaks on radio and John McCormack sings
And Patrick's Bell and shining swords salute the King of
kings

### Poor Clares
Poor Clare house in Dublin town
where prayer goes up and peace comes down
to heal the heart; and secular sounds
come in at times from the Horse Show grounds
My mother, bless her, loved the nuns
she'd get their prayers and bake them buns
they surely sensed, they surely knew
that she was good at praying too
I said the odd prayer there myself
had many a read at their booklet shelf

and priested, *Deo gratias*,
offered with them first holy Mass
Numen: a door, it seemed, on fire
holding the Host that faced the choir
Portiuncula: cool and high
a chapel where I'd like to die

### Assisi

Basilica: Giotto's mural art
and in the lower church its second heart
(the eucharistic Jesus is the first):
the bones of Francis locked and sealed in stone
lifted high as on a royal throne
a paradox for one whose only thirst
while still on earth was for the Crucified
sharing his hands and feet and open side

A very special eucharistic room
four small altars there around the tomb
Francis is the deacon, I the priest
a brother mingles work and ritual
I like to think that Francis serves as well
mystically sharing Gift and Feast
that I may love the wounded risen One
And bear whatever stigmata may come

### Lusaka

Faces black and brown and tan and white
come to share one Bread
theirs one radiant Light
'the queen of colours,' as Augustine said

Behind each face ancestral memories
cricket bats, hurleys, drums
islands in summer seas …
welcome from half the world to Him who comes

I move along, I'm learning quite a bit
the Life, the Love, the Body: this is it:
*Ecclesia*
*Catholica*

### Rift Valley

Small brown men from Italy
captured in the tide of war
by the cooler Englishry
built this church in Africa

They built the kind of church they knew
from floor to roof Italian-styled
with high-enthroned in blazing hue
Santa Maria and her Child

And there they went to Mass and prayer
while guards discreetly stood around
and through the Kenyan mountain air
they made a brave Italian sound

At last the soldiers went away
the wave of freedom rolled along
and now still browner people pray
and fill the church with Kenyan song

Mother and Child still guard the Rift
gaze on the mountains, scan the sky
as though they saw the primal drift
of hominids from Olduvai

### Bray Head

We found it there, Charlie my friend and I
on the edge of a Bray Head green where golf was played:
a tiny ancient ruined church: we prayed
imagined the scene of centuries gone by

Host and Cup to the east, to the rising sun
facing the sea where Patrick and others came
like them announcing the Spirit, the Power, the Name
Christ on the island edge of Christendom

### Arbour Hill

The one and only time I offered Mass in jail
so long ago: some memories linger, never fail
An Enniscorthy nation-guest was sacristan
Mass-accoutrements all shining, spick-and-span
I carefully chose Prayer number four with words to fit
its phrase 'to prisoners freedom' was quite apposite
I can't remember what I said in homily
(I could have said that Christ, a Prisoner, set us free)

warders, prisoners, full house, in faith all one
so many came to greet him in Communion

Where are they now? Still there, in death, in life-release?
May Arbour Hill be a waiting-post to God's own peace

### Mountjoy

A Mountjoy chaplain showed me chapel, sacristy
and then a room adjacent to the altar-space
'This was where a prisoner condemned to die
came to Mass: no chapel-folk could see his face
through a hatch he'd see and hear the priest at prayer
mutter the prayers he knew and, doubtless engraced, repent
and, if he so desired, the special moment came
the priest approached the hatch and gave the Sacrament'

I thought at first: a room to be frightened of
but now I know: a room of hope and love

### Nursing Home Mass

They come to Mass wheeled-in or limping, arm-assisted
aware, no doubt, that in the catalogue they're listed
as praying for the Church and their Society
(in terms of Christian thought a work of high degree)

No doubt too, they still recall the by-gone years
triumphs, failures, ups and downs, the hopes, the fears
and then at last the moment comes, the change occurs
in cowboy terms the deed is done: 'hang up your spurs'

They welcome Christ: they thank, adore their Lord and
King
He welcomes them, accepts their vow-made offering
He thanks them for their bearing, sharing Calvary's Cross
and promises He will walk with them to their Emmaus

*(This poem is dedicated to the patients and staff of
Cherryfield Nursing Home, Ranelagh, Dublin 6)*

# BIBLIOGRAPHY

New Testament quotations in the author's own text are from *The New Revised Standard Version* of the Holy Bible. Recent papal statements are given by permission of Libreria Editrice Vaticana. *The New Catholic Encyclopedia* was a source of brief data. The bibliography does not list works that are named in the first two chapters.

Abbott SJ, Walter and Gallagher, Monsignor Joseph, eds, *The Documents of Vatican II* (London: Geoffrey Chapman, 1966).

Bieler, Ludwig, *The Works of Saint Patrick* (London: Longmans, Green and Co., 1953).

*Corpus Scriptorum Ecclesiasticorum Latinorum,* Vol. 68, 1936.

De Foucauld, Blessed Charles, *Spiritual Autobiography*, Six, Jean-Francois, ed. and annot., Holland Smith, J., trans. (New Jersey: Dimension Books, 1964).

De Journal, Rouet, *Enchiridion Patristicum* (Frieburg im Breisgau: Herder, 1992).

De Lubac SJ, Henri, *The Faith of Teilhard de Chardin*, Hahue, René, trans. (London: Burns and Oates, 1965).

Denzinger-Bannwart, Heinrich-Cemens, *Enchiridion Symbolorum, Definitionum et Declarationum* (Frieburg im Breisgau: Herder, 1911).

Duffy, Eamon, *The Stripping of the Altars* (Newhaven and London: Yale University Press, 1992).

Ellis, John Tracy, *Documents of American Catholic History* (Milwaukee: Bruce Publishing House, 1962).

Flannery OP, Austin, ed., *Vatican II: Conciliar and Post-Conciliar Documents* (Dublin: Dominican Publications, 1996, published by Pillar Books by arrangement with Costello Publishing Company Inc.).

Guinness, Sir Alec, *Blessings in Disguise* (Middlesex, England: Penguin, 1997).

Martin, Saint Thérèse, *Poems*, Bancroft, Alan, trans. (London: Fount Harper Collins, 1996).

Merton OCSO, Thomas, *The Living Bread* (London: Burns and Oates, 1976).

Mitchell, Penny Blaker, *Mother Theodore Guérin A Woman for Our Time: Foundress of the Sisters of Providence of Saint Mary-of-the-Woods, Indiana* (Indiana: Sisters of Providence, 1998).

Moran, Patrick Francis, *History of the Catholic Church in Australasia* (Sydney: Oceanic Publishing Company, 1895).

Newman, Blessed John Henry, *Loss and Gain*, quoted in Brémond, Henri, *The Mystery of Newman* (London: Williams and Norgate, 1907).

Newman, Blessed John Henry, *Meditations and Devotions* (London: Longmans, Green and Co., 1963).

O'Connor, John, *A Moment of Grace* (San Francisco: Ignatius Press, 1995).

Ó Laoghaire SJ, Diarmuid, ed., *Ár bPaidreacha Dúchais* (Dublin: Foilseacháin Ábhair Spioradálta, 1982).

Opala ODC, Robert, 'Edith Stein and the Eucharist', *Carmelite Horizons* (Dublin: Irish Carmelite Communications, 2005).

O'Rahilly, Alfred, *Father William Doyle SJ* (London: Longmans, Green and Co., 1922).

Quasten, Johannes, *Patrology Volume 1* (Utrecht-Antwerp: Spectrum; Westminster, Maryland: Newman Press, 1962).

Redmond SJ, Stephen, *Faith of Two Peoples* (Dublin: Messenger Publications, 2004).

Redmond SJ, Stephen, *The Amazing Sacrament* (Dublin: Veritas, 2005).

Redmond SJ, Stephen, *Where Glory Dwells* (Dublin: Veritas, 2003).

Stein, Edith, *Essential Writings*, Sullivan ODC, John, ed. (New York, Maryknoll: Orbis Books, 2002).

Veritas, *The Veritas Hymnbook* (Dublin: Veritas, 1975).